CHARGING the HUMAN BATTERY

50 Ways to MOTIVATE Yourself

MAC ANDERSON

Published by Simple Truths, LLC
1952 McDowell Road, Suite 205
Naperville, IL 60563-65044

Design: Rich Nickel
Edited by: Stephanie Trannel

Printed and bound in China

ISBN 978-1-60810-017-0

simple truths®
THE GIFT OF INSPIRATION

www.simpletruths.com
(800) 900-3427

01 4CPG 09

Introduction

Motivation has always been a subject that has fascinated me. Why is it that some people, regardless of their circumstances, can stay energized and excited about life while others are controlled by their circumstances? I think that one of the greatest challenges in life is to get inside our own heads, and truly understand what makes us tick. It's not easy, but this little book was written with that in mind.

Self-motivation...what does it mean? There's a simple definition for a complex subject: **Self-motivation is an inner drive that compels behavior.** What makes it complex, however, is that little word "inner," because what works for me may not work for you, and vice-versa.

There are, however, some common denominators; some basic fundamentals when it comes to motivating ourselves. It's these fundamental ideas, and some other things that have worked for me personally, that I'd like to share with you. As we all know, it's not always what is said, but how it's said that can turn the switch from "off" to "on." One idea, if you're ready for it, can change your life forever.

Just remember...**people are like sticks of dynamite; the power's on the inside but nothing happens until the fuse gets lit.** It is my hope that as you read this book there will be many "a-ha moments" to light your fuse, and keep it lit, through good times and bad. But here's the key...keep it close and read it often. Because as my friend Zig Ziglar said, "People often tell me that motivation doesn't last, and I tell them, bathing doesn't either, that's why I recommend it daily!"

Live with Passion,

"Everything that's really worthwhile in life comes to us free – our minds, our souls, our bodies, our hopes, our dreams, our intelligence, our love of family and friends and country. All of these priceless possessions are free."

~Earl Nightingale

T

hink about it. You can lose all of your money and start over. If your house burns down, you can rebuild it. It's the things that cost you nothing that you can never replace.

One of the most important keys to self-motivation is to clearly identify your core values in life. You must decide what matters most. Why the need to identify your values? Many people think, "I know what's important, I don't need a list to remind me." What they don't fully understand, however, is that core values often serve as critical guides for making important decisions. When you're in doubt, your core values will cut through the fog like a beacon.

We all know there are many distractions along the road of life that will try to pull us away from our values. Sometimes we are forced to make difficult choices. But a good rule of thumb is that when you have to sacrifice material possessions for one of those "free things" that life has given you...you've made the right choice.

MOTIVATION
RECHARGEABLE

"You are always only one choice away from changing your life."

Think about that. One choice, just one, can change your life forever. Simply put, your life today is what your choices have made it, but with new choices, you can change directions this very moment. For me, that idea alone is highly motivational because it offers tremendous hope, regardless of circumstances, for a better tomorrow.

Your life changing choice may be to switch careers, to leave an abusive relationship, to go back to school, to stop drinking, to adopt a child, to start a business, to lose weight, to start a charity...to name a few. If you have the courage to do so, you could make any one of those choices, or others, today. And you would change your life.

Sometimes it's a different kind of choice. It can be to not quit, to not give up in the face of adversity. We've all been there.

Jack Canfield and Mark Victor Hansen received 77 rejections for their idea *Chicken Soup for the Soul*. They had to make a decision each time...should they throw in the towel and say enough is enough, or should they keep trying to pursue their dreams? You know the rest of the story. The 78th publisher said "Yes" and they went on to sell over 100 million books.

So never forget that you are only one choice away from changing your life. Do you have the courage to make it?

"Fear kills more people than death."

General George Patton

Master success coach, Steve Chandler said, "The world's best kept secret is that on the other side of your fear there is something safe and beneficial waiting for you. If you pass through even a thin curtain of fear you will increase the confidence you have in your ability to create your life."

Your ability to confront your fears is one of the most important keys to staying motivated. Because when you back away and do nothing, fear can quickly dominate your thinking and your emotions.

Everyone has fears and it takes courage to confront them. Mark Twain said, "Courage is resistance to fear, mastery of fear – not – absence of fear." When you're afraid, you have two choices: to do nothing and let fear fester like a cancer, or identify the person or situation that is causing your fear and deal with it immediately. Can it be difficult? Of course it can, but the alternative to constant worry and pain is much worse.

"You often hear,
'Be bold. Take a leap!'
Sometimes you should.
Other times, there's a
better idea. Take a step."

~Harry Beckwith

From his best-selling software to his blog, *Persistence Unlimited,* Brad Isaac lives goal setting. He describes how years ago when he was trying to learn the ropes as a comic, he met Jerry Seinfeld and asked him if he had any tips for a young comic. What Seinfeld told him he never forgot.

Seinfeld said that the way to be a better comic and create better jokes is to write every day. He said that he used a leverage technique to motivate himself even when he didn't feel like writing.

Here's how it worked...

Seinfeld told Brad to get a big wall calendar that has a whole year on one page and hang it on a prominent wall. He said each day that you write, put a big red X over that day. "After a few days", Seinfeld said, "you'll have a chain. Just keep at it, and the chain will grow longer each day. You'll enjoy seeing the chain when you get a few weeks under your belt. Now your only job is to not break the chain. Don't break the chain," he said again for emphasis.

This is great advice, not only for comics, but for anyone with a goal they wish to achieve. Daily action builds habits. It gives you practice and will keep you moving towards your goals. If you don't break the chain, you'll spot opportunities you otherwise wouldn't. All of the small improvements accumulate into large improvements rapidly because daily action provides "compounding interest."

"We first make our habits, and then our habits make us."

~John Dryden

"There is a remarkable difference between a commitment of 99% and 100%."

~Vic Conant

If you're married, your primary relationship in life is with your spouse. And of course, the strength of that relationship will go a long way to determine your happiness in life.

Vic Conant, the president of Nightingale Conant, has been a good friend for over twenty years. Not long ago he wrote an article called *The Keys to Successful Living* that focused on things we can do to improve our marriages. It was terrific!

Vic acknowledged that a few years ago he had some problems with his marriage to the point where he was considering other alternatives. But he wanted it to work and decided to try what he called "the 100% commitment experiment" (not 99%, but 100%). He said in doing so something magical happened. He began to look for the positives and began to enjoy his wife more each day. She naturally responded by being much nicer to him. He said it began an amazing transformation and today, after 36 years of marriage, they've never been happier.

As Vic discovered, there is a remarkable difference between a commitment of 99% and a commitment of 100%. At 100%, you are seeing your problems all the way through to their solutions. At 99% we can still find a way to take the path of least resistance...and usually do.

And guess what? "The 100% commitment experiment" not only works for marriage, it also works for life.

"True silence is to the spirit what sleep is to the body...nourishment and refreshment."

~William Penn

Solitude is a fundamental primordial need. In fact, I found it very interesting to read that all tribal cultures (including Native Americans) have an old ritual of going alone into the wilderness in search of clarity. They retreat from their daily lives to purify themselves and to renew their purpose and direction in life.

In today's world, whether we realize it or not, I think many of us are searching and longing for solitude. When it's been too long since I've had a break it begins to affect my moods, my energy levels, and my ability to think clearly and act decisively. My body, my mind and my soul are telling me to seek solitude.

To stay motivated, to keep your emotional battery charged, I highly recommend setting aside pockets of time during each day for solitude. You might have only five or ten minutes, but be alone and uninterrupted. And then sometime each week devote an extended time of one hour or more to reconnect with your soul. How and when you do it is a very personal thing, but plan it because solitude doesn't usually happen on its own. Make it a priority in your life.

#7

"Serve and grow rich."

Someone once said, "Life is like a game of tennis. The player who serves well seldom loses." Financial wealth can be fleeting, but what we do for others is lasting.

Serving others makes us feel good about ourselves because in our hearts we know it's the right thing to do. As Marian Wright said, "Service is the rent we pay for being. It is the very purpose of life, and not something you do in your spare time." Even the simplest gestures demonstrate this. Think about how you feel when you open a door for someone. They say, "Thank you." You say, "You're welcome." And your heart smiles. Why? Because you feel good about yourself. You did the right thing.

From day one at Simple Truths, my goal has been to create a "service culture." When we focus on serving the customer and serving each other, good things happen. We create a company of which we'll all be proud. Of course, everyone understands why we serve customers, since they pay the bills. But it's serving each other, with a smile in our hearts...that makes it a great place to work!

"Sometimes I get the feeling that the whole world is against me, but deep down I know that is not true. Some of the smaller countries are neutral."

-Robert Orben

think we've all had that feeling at some point in our lives. I know I have! Sometimes to stay motivated there's only one option: hang on until the storms blow through. In fact, if I could pick one word to describe any success I've enjoyed, I wouldn't hesitate; the word is perseverance. There have been a lot of potholes, roadblocks and detours along the way. As Leo Tolstoy said, **"The two most powerful warriors are patience and time."**

Over the years, when times got tough there has been one quote (and I love quotes) that has always gotten me through the adversity I was facing. It's such a simple thought, but it works magic in my brain. The quote is "Inch by inch, life's a cinch. Yard by yard, life is hard." I don't even know who said it first, but for me it simply means take a deep breath; make a list of the things you need to do; and start knocking them off one at a time.

So here's my challenge to you. Find your quote or a simple thought that keeps you motivated and use it to give you peace of mind when times get tough.

"He who has health has hope. And he who has hope has everything."

~Arabian Proverb

Abraham Heschel said, "Self-respect is the root of discipline; the sense of dignity grows with the ability to say no to oneself." More than anything, good health is the result of discipline and your ability to say "no" when you need to. Saying no to sleeping in when you could be exercising, saying no to the cheeseburger when it could be a salad, saying no to something that will add more stress to your life. No question about it...good health and discipline are joined at the hip.

In Brian Tracy's personal development seminars, he teaches the five "Ps" of excellent health. Read them often as a reminder of what it takes to stay healthy.

THE 5 Ps FOR GOOD HEALTH

1. Proper Exercise

The most important exercise for a long life is aerobic exercise. Walk, run, swim, etc., to get your heart rate up to a high level for at least thirty minutes three times a week.

2. Proper Diet

As Ben Franklin said, "Eat to live rather than live to eat." The keys, according to Tracy, are lean sources of protein, a variety of fruits and vegetables, and lots of water.

3. Proper Weight

You'll look good, feel good and feel more in control of your life when you're at a healthy weight.

4. Proper Rest

More than 60 percent of adults do not get enough sleep. Most people need eight hours a night. You also need regular breaks from work, both weekends and vacations.

5. Proper Attitude

This, according to Tracy, is perhaps the most important of all. The quality that is most predictive of health, happiness and long life is "optimism." The more optimistic you are about yourself and your life, the better your health in all areas.

So focus on the five "Ps" to stay healthy, stay happy and to stay motivated.

"Life can only be understood backwards; but it must be lived forward."

~Kierkegaard

Understanding that we control our own destiny is key to our success in life. Simply put, when we decide how we want our life to be we must take responsibility and move forward. Lance Wubbels has captured the essence of the "live life forward" idea with these simple but powerful affirmations:

From this moment forward...I stop the blame game and excuses. I am responsible for my life and for where I am today. I cannot blame the people and circumstances in my past, and I refuse to hide behind my past mistakes.

From this moment forward...I take responsibility for my thoughts, beliefs, decisions, and actions. If I am unhappy with something in my life, the power to change lies within me.

From this moment forward...I rid my soul of all bitterness, grudges, rage and anger against others. I will forgive others and stop wasting my life by trying to get even. I will be kind and compassionate to others.

From this moment forward...I will focus on knowing what I desire in life and let it light a fire under me. I want to run through life with passion.

So take a moment to write your own "From this moment forward." It takes courage, but it can change your life!

"The key to success in life is using the good thoughts of wise people."

~Leo Tolstoy

A fox, a wolf, and a bear went hunting and each got a deer. A discussion followed about how they should divide the spoils.

The bear asked the wolf how he thought it should be done. The wolf answered, "That's simple. Each of us should get one deer." As soon as the wolf finished speaking, the bear ate him.

Then the bear asked how the fox would divvy up the spoils. The fox offered his deer to the bear and suggested that he take the wolf's as well.

"Where did you get such wisdom?" asked the bear.

"From the wolf," replied the fox.

Sometimes in our life, there are no substitutes for experience. The problem is we rarely have it until after we need it.

The only way I know to advance the speed by which experience comes is to seek it from those who are wiser than we are. Many years ago I heard a quote that I never forgot. It said "You'll obtain more wisdom by spending an hour with a wise person than you'll gain by reading twenty books." I'm so glad that I heard it when I was young because all my life I've made a point to meet with successful people whenever possible. In fact, there were times that I went way out of my way to create the opportunity.

The biggest difference in meeting face-to-face versus reading a book is the privilege of asking questions and hearing answers. Answers to questions that pertain to your life, your goals and your dreams can make a very powerful impact on your thinking. The other big advantage to meeting a wise person is that it could be the beginning of an ongoing relationship that will allow you to seek more wisdom in the future.

"The years teach much which the days never knew."

~Ralph Waldo Emerson

"Most people are about as happy as they make up their minds to be."

"**W**ake up! If you knew for certain you had a terminal illness—if you had little time left...would you waste it? Well, I'm telling you that you do have a terminal illness. It's called birth. You don't have more than a few years left. No one does! So be happy now, without reason—or you never will be happy at all." What a great thought by Dan Millman from *The Way of the Peaceful Warrior.*

Wayne Dyer said, "There are two kinds of people in this world: ducks and eagles." We've all known ducks that quack a lot and constantly complain about their lot in life. But how refreshing it is when we meet an eagle who goes about their business and soars above the crowd.

I think Lincoln got it right...we are about as happy as we make up our minds to be!

"Expect the unexpected."

heard a great story recently about a guy who decided to send flowers to the grand opening of a friend's restaurant. At the grand opening, he decided to check out the flowers he'd sent. Much to his dismay, he discovered that he'd sent a white wreath that said, "May you rest in peace." Of course, he panicked and steped out to call his florist. The florist said, "Bob, I'm not worried about you because as we speak, there's a guy being buried who got a dozen roses that said, "Good luck in your new location!"

For sure, life can throw us a curve ball when we least expect it. It's not a matter of if, but when. And there's always a little comfort in a "Plan B."

Your future doesn't usually happen by accident and when you think about it, it's all you've got. A well-thought out plan for your life improves your confidence, increases your levels of motivation and lowers your stress. And while you're at it, spend a little time on your "Plan B."

"When we listen, really listen deeply, something shifts during communication."

~Steve Shapiro

You might be thinking, "What does listening have to do with self-motivation?" The answer...a lot! Being a great listener is key to building great relationships, and great relationships keep us happy, healthy and motivated. Why is that? Feeling appreciated, wanted and loved are powerful human needs and that is what relationships give us. They build our self-worth and self-image both of which are critical to staying positive and motivated.

Think for a minute about the friends you really enjoy being with (I mean really enjoy). I'd be willing to bet they are great listeners. So never forget that your ability to listen, more than any other factor, determines the quality of your communication. The quality of your communication determines, more than any other factor, the quality of your relationship. And the quality of your relationships, more than any other factor, determines the quality of your life.

"You can't believe how hard it is for people to be simple, how much they fear being simple. They worry that if they're simple, people will think they're simpleminded. In reality, of course, it's just the reverse."

-Jack Welch

This is a quote from Jack Welch, one of the great business leaders of our generation. As the CEO of General Electric, he reinvented the company and made it one of the most respected companies in the world. How did he do it? He simplified his business model and reinforced his goals every chance he had. Focus and effective communication were the keys to his success.

So here's the question: **If a leader like Jack Welch understands the awesome power of simplicity, why doesn't the rest of the world?**

As it relates to self-motivation, the power of simplicity and focus is critical. In business and in life, there is the tendency to think that "more is better." And I must admit I fell into that trap early in my career. But as I've gotten older, and hopefully a little wiser, I've made a u-turn. I now realize that to accomplish more, I must focus on less. In fact, this realization was the driving force behind our company, which is appropriately named "Simple Truths." My goal was to have engaging content that could be read in about thirty minutes. In other words, not all you need to know about a topic, but the most important things you need to know.

In the end, self-motivation comes easy if you are "focused on the critical few and not the insignificant many." Keep your mind clear and uncluttered; your energy levels are higher when you are focused on what matters most.

16

"No one would have crossed the ocean if he could have gotten off the ship in the storm."

~Charles Kettering

The path of least resistance is always very tempting, and we all need shots of inspiration from time to time to get off of it and make our own path. For me, the inspiration can come from people I've read about who kept going and succeeded against all odds. People who had every reason to quit but chose to place their dreams above their fears. For example:

One of the great American novelists, Jack London, received 600 rejection notices from publishers before he sold his first book. Can you image? Six hundred "nos" before getting a "yes"!

Ray Kroc, at the age of 52, talked to over one hundred investors over a two year period before he got the money for a crazy idea called...McDonalds!

Helen Keller had every reason in the world to give up, but chose not to; and as a result inspired millions of people around the world.

Thomas Edison had 1,093 patents in his name – more than any other American in history. He had this to say about staying power:

"If I find 10,000 ways something won't work, I haven't failed. I am not discouraged, because every wrong attempt discarded is often a step forward."

Margaret Thatcher, the first woman prime minister of Great Britain, said it best.

"You may have to fight a battle more than once to win it."

"The difference in winning or losing is most often... not quitting."

~Walt Disney

17

"Life engenders life.
Energy creates energy.
It is by spending oneself
that one becomes rich."

Sarah Bernhardt's quote is about passion. When we become passionate about something good, our life becomes richer for it.

Hank Haney is the golf coach for Tiger Woods. Of course, he has a lot of parents requesting him to teach their childern how to play like Tiger. He tells them that their goal is a bit unrealistic because, in his words, "There probably won't be another Tiger Woods in our lifetime."

But he does take new students and the key to their success, he says, is their passion for the game. It's more about passion than talent; it's more about reaching potential than being gifted.

Everyone has unique God-given talents. But from time to time, you must step up to the mirror and ask yourself a very important question. "Are you doing all you can do to become all you can be?" Your level of motivation, many times, can be traced back to your answer to that one question. If you become passionate about reaching your full potential, you can't help but stay motivated.

True passion originates in our soul. Ignite it! Ferdinand Foch said, **"The most powerful weapon on earth is the human soul on fire."**

18

"Laughter is an
instant vacation."

~Milton Berle

Sometimes a little humor can create an "A ha" moment. A few weeks ago a friend sent me an email and said, "Mac, I think you'll like this." He was right. I did. It not only made me smile, but made me think...a good combination! So here it is. Some simple life lessons from *Everything I Need to Know About Life I Learned From Noah's Ark*.

~ Don't miss the boat

~ Remember, we're all in the same boat

~ Plan ahead

~ Stay fit
(when you're 600 years old someone may ask you to do something really big)

~ Don't listen to critics; just get on with the job that needs to be done

~ Build your future on high ground

~ For safety's sake, travel in pairs

~ Speed isn't always an advantage
(the snails were on board with the cheetahs)

~ When you're stressed, float for awhile

~ Remember the ark was built by amateurs, and the Titanic, by professionals

~ And just one more thing... the woodpecker might have to go!

19

"Some stress is unavoidable, some is not. The trick is learning to distinguish between the two."

~Dr. Paul Rosch

Stress, and how we deal with it, is a big factor in staying motivated. I read a great article recently in *Mens Health* magazine titled: *Break the Stress Cycle… Separate the Stressors From the Energizers*. It offers some simple, great advice on dealing with stress.

Some stress is unavoidable. Some is not. "The trick is learning to distinguish between the two," says Paul Rosch, M.D., president of the American Institute of Stress. He can't identify your sources of stress for you, because one man's stress is another man's joy. So you'll have to do that part yourself. Divide your stresses into two lists: "accept" and "change."

As you draw up your lists, you'll naturally pay attention to what your brain knows about your sources of stress, but make sure you listen to your body's complaints as well. When are you experiencing those headaches? Or back pain? Is there a pattern to your heartburn, or a particular stretch of your commute that provokes road rage? "Learn how your body responds so you can detect early warning signs of stress," says Dr. Rosch.

In evaluating your stressors, do sweat the small stuff. It's the petty problems that cause serious stress in the long run, says Harvard psychologist Daniel Gilbert, Ph.D. Having to listen to your girlfriend's Jimmy Buffet CDs night after night really could push you over the edge. (But not into Margaritaville.)

Your activities during these first 7 days are not merely a prelude. **Simply sitting down to identify all the things that stress you out, and deciding to do something about them, is a powerful stress buster in itself.** It's been known since the 1950s that stress is exacerbated if a person has no sense of control and no hope that things will get better.

Having goals, and reaching those goals, is the healthy opposite of that. "Too often, we are adrift on the sea of life," says Dr. Rosch.

Drop anchor.

"The most important thing about goals is having one."

~Geoffrey Abert

20

"What a man thinks of himself, that is which determines, or rather indicates, his fate."

~Henry David Thoreau

John Maxwell in his book, *The Difference Maker,* said, "How you see yourself has a tremendous impact on your attitude. Poor self-images and poor attitudes often walk hand-in-hand. It's hard to see the world as positive if you see yourself as negative."

Dr. Wayne Dyer tells us to examine the labels we apply to ourselves. He said, "Every label is a boundary or limit you will not let yourself cross." You may not even be conscious of what labels you apply, or they may be labels left over from childhood.

Ken Blanchard said, "I go out into the world every day with the attitude that my 'okayness' is not up for grabs. That doesn't mean I don't have areas of my life that need improvement — just that at my basic core, I'm okay. If people give me negative feedback, or criticize something I do, my self-esteem permits me to listen in a non-defensive way — looking to see if there is something I can learn."

Norman Vincent Peale said, "We have two choices every day. We can feel good about ourselves or we can feel lousy...why would anyone choose the latter?"

21

"How far you go in life
depends upon your being...
tender with the young
compassionate with the aged
sympathetic with the striving
tolerant of the weak
and the strong
because...
some day in your life,
you will have been
all of these."

~George Washington Carver

This is one of my all-time favorite quotes because it captures the essence of a life well-lived. It also captures the essence of kindness.

You may be wondering, "What in the world does kindness have to do with self-motivation?" There is a beautiful poem titled WINNING, that gives you the answer...

Winning is giving your best self away
Winning is serving with grace every day.

You'll know that you've won when your friends say it's true,
"I like who I am, when I'm around you."

You look for the best in the others you see
And you help us become who we're trying to be.

Winning is helping someone who's down
It's sharing a smile instead of a frown.

It's giving your children a hug by the fire
And sharing the values and dreams that inspire.

It's giving your parents the message, "I care.
Thanks, Mom and Dad, for being so fair."

Winners are willing to give more than get
Their favors are free, you're never in debt.

Winners respect every color and creed
They share and they care for everyone's need.

The losers keep betting that winning is getting
But there's one of God's laws that they keep forgetting.

And this is the law you can live and believe
The more that you give, the more you'll receive.

~Author Unknown

"We make a living by what we get. We make a life by what we give."

~Winston Churchill

22

"People often tell me, 'You know, Zig, motivation doesn't last,' and I say... bathing doesn't either, that's why I recommend it daily."

n my book, *The Power of Attitude*, I share the fact that some people think that because I am who I am, I'm always positive. They think, "You started Successories. You couldn't possibly have a negative thought." Well, here's a confession. One of the main reasons I started Successories is that I needed continuous reinforcement to keep me motivated and focused on my goals. In a perfect world, we hear something once, and don't need to hear it again. Well, I don't know where you live, but my world is far from perfect. I occasionally have doubts, fears and disappointments in my life, and I need "shots of inspiration" to encourage me and keep me motivated.

If staying positive and motivated is really important to you, you'll be proactive and develop a plan to reinforce your attitude on a daily, weekly and monthly basis. But if you think it'll happen on its own, you're wrong. What works best for each of us is a very personal thing. It could be inspirational books, or CDs, prayer, music, or having regular conversations with a positive friend. But here's the key...don't wait until you're down to act. Put your plan in place today to help keep your attitude on the right track.

23

"If I really want to improve
my situation, I can work on
the one thing over which
I have control — myself."

Stephen R. Covey

Ben Franklin said, "An investment in knowledge always pays the best interest." To stay motivated, to improve your situation, you must continue to grow and learn. Knowledge is the only way to keep gas in your tank.

My challenge for you is simple. Identify a goal that is important. It could be starting your own business. It could be improving skills at your existing job. Or it could be more personal, such as being a better parent, or being a better spouse. Once you've identified your goal, I challenge you to spend thirty minutes a day seeking knowledge and clarity on the goal you've selected. If you have the discipline to do it, this simple exercise can change your life. Knowledge, you'll find, is power. It will give you the self-confidence to make difficult choices and to continuously move forward toward your goals.

"I'm not afraid of storms, for I'm learning how to sail my ship."

~Louisa May Alcott

24

"Courage is a door
that can only be opened
from the inside."

~Terry Neil

recently read an article in *USA Today* about Mark Speckman. The headline read, *"A Small-Time Coach With a Big-Time Message."* The article, written by David Moore, started by saying, "The Willamette University football team is in good hands, even though their coach was born without them."

His players love him. He has a great sense of humor about his disability, and he wins...consistently. Of course, there are things that Speckman can't do like tying his shoes. He has succeeded in life, he says, by always saying, "There's always a way...figure it out." When he was young his mom didn't coddle him and would come up with little tests like changing the light bulbs just to see if he could do it.

He always has found a way, it seems. He became a college football player (Honorable mention All-American), a trombone player (an instrument with no fingering), a college graduate, a high school teacher, and a great coach who is respected and admired by his players. Tim Alton, a 21 year old senior free safety who aspires to become a doctor, said this about Coach Speckman: "At the beginning of the season, we're worried about two-a-day practices. We're tired. We're dragging. Then we look over at our coach and he has no hands. It's pretty hard to feel sorry for yourself."

Eleanor Roosevelt would have respected Mark Speckman's resolve. It was she who said,

"We must do the things we think we cannot do."

"Courage is the finest of human qualities because it is the quality which guarantees all the others."

~Winston Churchill

#25

"Change comes
bearing gifts."

~Price Pritchett

Comfort zones put padlocks on doors to growth, discovery and adventure. As painful as it may feel, change almost always comes bearing gifts. As nerve-wracking as it can seem, it's "in the winds of change we find our true direction."

Change is not easy, but it is simple. Things will always change. We don't have a choice about that. But we do have a choice about how we react to change. It really boils down to this...either we manage change, or it will manage us.

In the long run, however, sameness is the fast track to mediocrity. To grow, to get closer to your goals, you must get off the path of least resistance. Lace up your running shoes, tie a double knot, and discover all the advantages you can uncover on a new trail.

"To get what you've never had, you must do what you've never done."

26

"Problems are opportunities in work clothes."

~Unknown

Someone once asked Norman Vincent Peale, "Don't you think life would be better if we had fewer problems?" Peale said, "I'll be happy to take you to Woodlawn Cemetery because the only people I know who don't have any problems are dead."

No question about it.

If your life doesn't have problems, you don't have a life.

The point is we can't avoid problems, so we might as well expect them and embrace them as opportunities to learn and grow.

In John Maxwell's book, *The Difference Maker*, he said twenty five years ago he wrote something that helped him see problems in a different light. It also helped me and I'd like to share it with you...

PREDICTORS – helping to mold our future

REMINDERS – showing us we can't succeed alone

OPPORTUNITIES – pulling us out of ruts and prompting
us to think creatively

BLESSINGS – opening doors we would otherwise
not go through

LESSONS – providing instruction with each new challenge

EVERYWHERE – telling us no one is excluded from difficulties

MESSAGES – warning us of potential disasters

SOLVABLE – reminding us that every problem has a solution

"Life is not about waiting for the storms to pass... it's about learning how to dance in the rain."

~Unknown

27

"When we choose not to focus on what is missing from our lives, but are grateful for the abundance that is present... we experience heaven on earth."

Betty Mahalik, in her book, *Living a Five Star Life,* asks the question: Where are you right now on the "joy factor" scale...more joy than you can handle, or barely enough to keep you alive? She said, "We live in times that are often a tumultuous combination of terror, anxiety and a realization of the fragility of life."

"Joy and gratitude," Betty says, "go hand in hand. We are not grateful because we're happy, rather we're happy because we're grateful." This week, she says, "Take five minutes a day to practice gratitude. As you look around, remember just how much you have to be thankful for – freedom, your faith, your friendships, your family, and the list goes on. You'll discover the world, that only yesterday seemed drab and joyless, is suddenly bursting with beauty and possibility."

Living with gratitude...ah, yes, easy to say, it just rolls off the tongue, but difficult to do consistently. You are so blessed, in so many ways. You need to find ways to remind yourself just how fortunate you really are. When that happens you will, as Sarah Breathnach says, "Experience heaven on earth."

28

"You can't hit a target
you can't see."

~Brian Tracy

You already know that it's important to set clearly defined and realistic goals for yourself. You also know that it's critical to work towards them every day. These two steps are key to providing clarity and focus in your life. What you may not realize is how important it is to put pen to paper (or fingers to keyboard).

USA Today did a recent study where researchers tracked individuals who made New Year's resolutions. They divided them into two groups: *(1) Those who made a New Year's resolution and wrote it down, and (2) those who made one but neglected to write it down.* The results were astonishing! Of those people who neglected to put their goal in writing, only 4% kept their resolution, however, of those people that wrote down their resolution, 44% had kept them.

In other words, your odds for success are increased ten fold by taking just a few minutes to put your goal in writing. With the stroke of a pen, it goes from being a wish...to a commitment.

29

"Feedback is the breakfast
of champions."

~Rich Tate

To grow, to become all we can be, we need honest feedback from people who care about us. For example, we may think we're on track to accomplish our goals, but somewhere along the way we missed a turn. We need, as Ken Blanchard calls them, "trusted truth tellers to tell us to back up, and head in the other direction."

Some people have a difficult time handling constructive criticism. As an entrepreneur, I've always welcomed honest feedback and disagreement from anyone on my team. In fact, another one of my favorite quotes is:

"In business, if two people always agree... one of them is unnecessary."

So invite, even cherish, feedback from your "trusted truth tellers." They may be your spouse, your parents, your friends, your mentors or co-workers that will offer their opinions.

Here are some examples of the questions you may wish to ask:

What are my strengths and weaknesses?

Are my goals realistic?

Am I headed in the right direction?

What do I need to improve?

What mentors do I know that could help me?

The answers to these questions may not always be what you wanted to hear, but they very well could be what you needed to hear.

"A true friend is somebody who can make us do what we can."

~Ralph Waldo Emerson

30

"Find what makes
your heart sing and create
your own music."

~M. Anderson

One of life's greatest challenges is to find your true purpose in life. As Confucius said many years ago, "Choose work that you love, and you'll never have to work another day in your life."

I feel that way. I pinch myself every day to make sure I'm not living a dream. I am so blessed to have the opportunity to create inspirational books and short inspirational movies that reinforce core values. We get wonderful feedback daily from people thanking us for making a difference and I never tire of hearing it. I'm always excited to wake up in the morning and work at something that I love doing.

It's not always easy to find your life's calling. Sometimes we find it through trial and error. But always remember, it's never too late. Ray Kroc, for example, founded McDonalds at age 52. I know many people who have decided to go back to school in their 60s and 70s. I know someone who, in her 50s, made the decision to move to India to start an orphanage. She said it was the best thing she has ever done. It is never too late to find your purpose and your passion in life.

We are all unique beings, with different interests and different talents. Discover your gifts, discover what moves you. Find what makes your heart sing.

It may take a lifetime, but it'll be worth the effort.

31

"Motives are like the rudder of a boat. The motor moves the boat, but if the rudder is just slightly set at the wrong angle...well, you can end up in the wrong place."

~John Blumberg

John Blumberg is a speaker and a friend. I love the way he writes and always look forward to receiving his monthly newsletter called *The Front Porch*. I'd like to share the one sent last month titled: *Motives of the Mind* written to help us understand what drives our motivation.

The real motor to our motivation is our motives. Motives are the deep-seeded driving forces that crank-up our motivation.

Motive sits at the beginning of motivation.

Literally....and in reality. Webster describes "motive" as something (a need or desire) that causes a person to act.

Our motivation can often be seen by others. It might be in our enthusiasm or in our endurance and persistence. Lack of motivation can be seen as well. But true motives are different. They are hard, if not impossible, to see in others. And it is often hard to see it in ourselves...especially when we don't really think about it.

Motives are tricky and can take on a life of their own. Have you ever been motivated to accomplish something by incredibly pure motives only to get side-tracked by selfish ones? These evasive, misguided motives might have been about getting your way or proving you were right. They might have been about pulling-rank or forcing your position on others. Left unchecked, your motives may be robbing you of your greatest performances and contributions.

So how often do you ask yourself the question, "What are my motives here? Are they pure or are they misguided?" This question, when answered honestly, will tell you if you're on the right course, or if your "rudder" needs to be turned in another direction.

"The heart knows, the heart knows... listen to your heart."

~Kathy Sherman

32

"Failure is only the opportunity to begin again more intelligently."

If you're going to take risks in life (and I highly recommend it if you want to grow), you will occasionally fail. It's not a matter of if, but a matter of when. It may be a failed relationship, a failed business, a failed career, or whatever. But this much is certain...you will at times fail.

So here's the deal. If you're going to fail, why not fail forward? Why not, as Henry Ford suggested, consider it as an opportunity to begin again more intelligently?

For me there has always been something comforting about that thought. When I'm making a decision that might involve risk (and as a life-long entrepreneur, I've made a few) it's comforting to know that if I fail, I'll learn something and move forward. Without question, my willingness to take calculated risks that I believe in has been the key to any success I've enjoyed in my business career. There were a lot of doubters who said that Successories and Simple Truths would never work. And although it was somewhat painful at times getting through the "learning curve," my belief never wavered. Were there failures along the way? Of course there were. But I always took Henry's advice and began again...more intelligently.

33

"Be glad you are you."

~Maureen Weiner

Ah, yes. There is something magical about an attitude of gratitude, and for me, there is also something magical in the words below. To stay motivated we all need sources of inspiration. Something we can turn to when we need a lift. Following is one of mine that I feel truly captures the essence of success. It was written by Australian Maureen Weiner. Enjoy!

Faith is a seed — plant it in your heart, tend it
with love and honesty, and watch it grow.
Treasure the gifts you have been given — you are
a miracle of creation.
Be noble in all you do, and remember that true
happiness comes from giving.
Embrace peace and compassion, and you will
know only joy. Love, understanding, and kindness

cost nothing and yet they are priceless. Give of

them generously and they will be returned to you

tenfold. They are qualities which never fade and

never age, but blossom with use.

Walk away from anger, retiring to the stillness

that lies within, harbouring peace and goodwill.

Let your thoughts be beautiful – they hold the

greatest power.

There is nothing you cannot achieve; whatever

you desire is in your reach.

And be glad you are you.

Let these words sink into your heart. Make them a part of your daily life.

Keep them close and read them often.

"What lies behind us, and what lies before us, are tiny matters compared to what lies within us."

~Ralph Waldo Emerson

34

"You become what you think about."

~Earl Nightingale

When I first heard Earl Nightingale's famous essay, *The Strangest Secret,* I was a sophomore in college and it changed my life forever. It is composed of approximately 5,000 words; and in those words was more wisdom, more common sense and more inspiration than in anything I had ever heard. From that point on, I've used Nightingale's message to keep me focused and motivated in good times and in bad. And I'm not alone. The essay has inspired millions around the world. In fact, it was the first non-musical recording to sell over one million copies. Here's a brief excerpt...

George Bernard Shaw said, "People are always blaming their circumstances for what they are. I don't believe in circumstances. The people who get on in this world are the people who get up and look for the circumstances they want, and if they can't find them, make them."

Now it stands to reason that a person who is thinking about a concrete and worthwhile goal is going to reach it, because that's what he's thinking about. And we become what we think.

Conversely, the person who has no goal, who doesn't know where he's going, and whose thoughts must therefore be thoughts of confusion, anxiety, fear and worry — his life becomes one of frustration, fear, anxiety and worry. And if he thinks about nothing...he becomes nothing.

Do yourself a favor. Read or listen to *The Strangest Secret* in its entirety. It will change the way you think about your life.

"Every thought is a seed.
If you plant crab apples,
don't count on harvesting
golden delicious."

~Bill Meyer

35

"Our doubts are traitors, and make us lose the good we oft might win by fearing to attempt."

~William Shakespeare

William James, one of the founders of modern psychology, said, "One of the greatest discoveries of our generation is that we can alter our lives by altering our attitudes." We all have that choice. We can choose to be positive and optimistic about life; or we can choose to be negative and pessimistic.

Dr. Norman Vincent Peale said that his greatest discovery in life, outside his relationship with God, was, "If you think in negative terms, you will get negative results. If you think in positive terms, you'll get positive results." He said, "This simple fact is the basis of an astonishing law of prosperity and success. In three words:

believe and succeed."

Sometimes in life we think something is too simple to be important. We hear it and say, "That's nice," and go about our business. But hearing and understanding — I mean truly understanding, are as different as night and day. If you truly understand this simple law of prosperity, it can change your attitude forever.

36

"If you advance confidently in the direction of your dreams and endeavor to live the life which you have imagined, you will meet with success unexpected in common hours."

~Henry David Thoreau

Your dreams are the blueprints of your soul. They should take you by the hand and lead you toward your life's purpose and passion. They are one of, if not the greatest, source of self-motivation that you have. So nurture them and feed them inspiration whenever you can.

Here's another beautiful poem by Maureen Weiner that will provide just that...

Build your castles in the air.

Set no limits.

Lay your foundations in the clouds.

You are the builder.

Color your life with the pictures in your mind.

Set no boundaries.

Let your imagination be the canvas.

You are the artist.

Find knowledge in the Universe.

Set no obstacle.

Life is your classroom.

You are the teacher.

Your dreams are your realities.

Dream on.

And let your spirits soar.

If you can see it, you can have it.

If you can feel it, you can be it.

If you can dream it, you can achieve it.

Dream on.

"To dream anything that you want to dream; that is the beauty of the human mind. To do anything you want to do; that is the strength of the human will. To trust yourself to test your limits; that is the courage to succeed."

~Bernard Edmonds

37

"Manage stress before
it manages you."

could never write a book on self-motivation without discussing the importance of regular exercise. In fact, I can be doing everything else right, but without regular exercise, my attitude and energy levels will head south.

For years, early in my career, I couldn't find the time. In hindsight, I didn't make the time because I didn't consider exercise a priority. It was an amazing discovery to find out what a positive difference it made in my life. My creativity improved, my energy levels shot up, my attitude stayed right and my problem solving abilities improved.

Exercise is also an excellent "stress buster." Don't kid yourself; stress is a killer. In fact, the World Health Association estimates that 80% of all illnesses are directly or indirectly caused by stress. Therefore, if you're not proactive in busting stress, it'll come back and bust you!

Thirty to forty-five minutes a day, three to four days a week; exercise is one of the best investments you can make to ensure a healthy body and a positive attitude.

38

"To carry a grudge is like being stung to death by one bee."

Hate, anger and resentment are like cancers and when you let them fester, they put an invisible ceiling on your future. When it comes to self-motivation, these thoughts can be public enemy #1.

In *The Power of Attitude*, I shared that there have been a few times in my life that I felt greatly wronged and taken advantage of. My first reaction, of course, was anger and resentment. I held it for awhile and felt my stomach tie up in knots, my appetite wane, and the joy slip out of my life. Then I read a quote from William Ward and the light bulb went on! He said, "Forgiveness is the key that unlocks the handcuffs of hate."

I thought...he's so right. It's time to forgive, to take off the handcuffs and move on with my life. From that moment on, everything seemed to change. The joy and peace of mind that I had lost slipped back into my life.

It was like I'd been playing the first half of a basketball game wearing three pound shoes, and at half-time the coach said, "Mac, put on these new Nikes for the second half."

"Forgiveness does not change the past, but it does enlarge your future."

~Paul Boese

Practice forgiveness and make your future longer than you ever imagined.

39

"In the race to be better
and best, lest we forget
to just be."

~Unknown

Just being...what a wonderful way of saying, STOP, and take time for today. Saturate yourself in the time you've been given right here, right now. Because you know what? This moment, right now, is unique to your life and you can never come back to it.

When our life is in its final hours, will we regret not taking more time for "just being?" Just being there to savor more sunsets; just being alone with our thoughts; just being surrounded by beautiful music; or just being with those we love so dearly.

If you have read the following poem, you know it's worth re-reading...often.

First I was dying to finish high school and start college.

And then I was dying to finish college and start working.

And then I was dying to marry and have children.

And then I was dying for my children

to grow old enough so I could go back to work.

And then I was dying to retire.

And now I am dying...

and suddenly realize that I forgot to live.

~Source Unknown

"Life must be lived as play."

~Plato

40

"Commitment is a line you cross. It is the difference between wishing and doing."

~Unknown

Commitment leads to action. Wishing leads to more wishing. Best-selling author Harry Beckwith wrote, "It's tempting to sit and wait for life to come to you. But it can't. It's too busy. Life is out there. You have to go for it."

Any successful person I've ever known has been willing to take action. There are a lot of people who dream about what they are going to do, but only a few actually step up to the plate and do it.

I love Wayne Gretsky's quote, "You miss 100% of the shots you don't take." If you believe something with all your heart, you must find the courage to follow your heart, or you'll live with regrets for the rest of your life.

I'll end this chapter with a short, but powerful quote from Peter Zarlenga. Three life-changing words...

"Action conquers fear."

41

"Look at everything as though you are seeing it for the first time, with the eyes of a child, fresh with wonder."

~Joseph Cornell

Chuck Bokar is a good friend and one of the most motivated people I know. His enthusiasm is infectious and he's always looking for new things to learn and ways to improve. One of his secrets to success is that he lives in awe. For Chuck, every new day is a masterpiece. He believes that life is now...this very moment. And he savors every moment of it. He, as Joseph Cornell's quote says, "Looks at life as would a child, fresh with wonder."

In 1993, North Carolina basketball coach, Jim Valvano was awarded the Arthur Ashe Award for Courage. He had recently discovered that he had incurable cancer and had been given six months to live. He ended his acceptance speech with these words:

"I urge all of you to enjoy your life, every precious moment on this earth. Spend each day with some laughter. Don't be afraid to feel...to get your emotions going. Be enthusiastic, because nothing great can be accomplished without enthusiasm. Live your dreams."

I have Valvano's words in my wallet to remind me to live in awe!

42

"The hardest arithmetic to master is that which enables us to count our blessings."

According to legend, a young man roaming the desert came across a spring of delicious crystal-clear water. The water was so sweet he filled his leather canteen so he could bring some back to a tribal elder who had been his teacher. After a four-day journey he presented the water to the old man who took a deep drink, smiled warmly, and thanked his student lavishly for the sweet water. The young man returned to his village with a happy heart.

Later, the teacher let another student taste the water. He spat it out, saying it was awful. It apparently had become stale because of the old leather container. The student challenged his teacher: "Master, the water was foul. Why did you pretend to like it?"

The teacher replied, "You only tasted the water. I tasted the gift. The water was simply the container for an act of living-kindness and nothing could be sweeter."

Self-motivation without gratitude is impossible. Our energy is "sapped" when our entire focus is on what's wrong instead of what is right with our lives. One of our greatest challenges is to live and love in spite of pain and disappointment...to find gratitude in the midst of it all.

"When it comes to life the critical thing is whether you take things for granted or take them with gratitude."

~G.K. Chesterton

Reflect for a moment on this beautiful quote from Melody Beattie:

"Gratitude unlocks the fullness of life. It turns what we have into enough, and more. It turns denial into acceptance, chaos to order, confusion to clarity. It can turn a meal into a feast, a house into a home, a stranger into a friend. Gratitude makes sense of our past, brings peace for today, and creates a vision for tomorrow."

#43

"The journey of a thousand miles begins with a single step."

-Lao Tzu

True...but that pesky first step can be a killer, can't it! I love Will Rogers' quote, "Even if you are on the right track, you'll get run over if you just sit there." So many times we have great intentions. We're going to read a good book, write out our five year life plan, start a new business, lose weight. But for some reason, we can't quite get around to taking that first step.

We're all guilty of procrastinating. But here's the thing. Procrastinating when something is important, when it's something you know you should do, can drain your energy and you won't even know it.

"Procrastination is attitude's natural assassin. There's nothing so fatiguing as an uncompleted task."

This quote by William James is worth its weight in gold. There are times when I have difficulty setting aside blocks of time to write. I know I should be doing it. In fact, I even love doing it (once I get started), but...here we go...back to that pesky first step.

When I need a "nudge," I visualize just how good I'm going to feel about myself when I finish. I know I'll feel energized. I also know I'll feel proud that I did something I didn't want to do.

So make a point to find that something that works for you when you need a nudge to get started.

44

"Any time a thought, sentence, or paragraph inspires you or opens up your thinking, you need to capture it, like a butterfly in a net, and later release it into your own field of consciousness."

~Steve Chandler

Chandler's quote captures the essence of the logic behind Successories. I thought, people want to decorate their walls, right? Why not do it with great ideas that reinforce what they believe? It was a simple idea, but unbelievably, no one had ever done it!

We live in a very busy, very cluttered world with a lot of decisions to make each day. It's easy to forget what's most important, unless we find ways to remind ourselves. For example, Arnold Schwarzenegger grew up in a poor town in Austria. His father framed and hung these simple words,

"Joy through Strength."

Schwarzenegger said that this single phrase made a big impact on his life. Earlier in this book, I shared how twelve little words had made a difference for me. When I was facing adversity in my life I always reminded myself, "Inch by inch, life's a cinch; and yard by yard, life is hard." For me, those words were always comforting and gave me courage to move forward. What thought works for you?

45

"Excuses are the nails used to build a house of failure."

~Don Wilder

William Henley said, "I am the master of my fate. I am the captain of my soul." Once you believe this (I mean, really believe it,) nothing will hold you back.

Something unexplainable happens when we accept complete responsibility for our behavior and our results. But it's not an easy thing to do. In my book, *Change is Good...You Go First,* I share some times in my life when my business was struggling and I found myself blaming others, blaming the economy, blaming this, blaming that! But as I've gotten a little older, and hopefully wiser, I've come to realize that when things go wrong in my business, or in my life, I can always find the culprit...in the mirror.

In every instance, it always comes back to to decisions I've made. Decisions that put me exactly where I was then and where I am today. This one "tweak" in my attitude may sound like a little thing, but it has made a big difference in my life.

46

"When we have done our best, we can await the results in peace."

~Unknown

I don't know who said this, but I do know that they were right on target. Let's take goals, for example. We set goals to keep us focused on the important things in our life; personal goals, career goals, spiritual goals, family goals, health goals, etc. Sometimes we set out with great enthusiasm to reach these goals, but occasionally there are circumstances that set us back. Some within our control...some not. But there is a wonderful feeling of peace when I know in my heart that I've done my best. Because, win or lose, I know that I'm more prepared for my next battle in life.

Committing to excellence is not an act, it's an attitude. It's an attitude that is captured in this short thought titled: *And Then Some...*

"And then some...
these three little words are the secret to success.
They are the difference between average people and top
people in most companies.
The top people always do what is expected...
and then some.
They are thoughtful of others; they are considerate
and kind...and then some.
They meet their responsibilities fairly and squarely...
and then some.
They are good friends and helpful neighbors...
and then some.
They can be counted on in an emergency...
and then some.
I am thankful for people like this, for they make
the world a better place. Their spirit of service is
summed up in these three little words...
and then some."

If we carry the attitude of *"And Then Some"*... throughout our life, when

our time on earth is almost gone, we will wait the results in peace.

"Give the world the best you have and the best will come back to you."

~Madeline Bridges

47

"No steam or gas drives anything until it is confined. No Niagara is ever turned into light and power until it is tunneled. No life ever grows great until it is focused, dedicated, disciplined."

Self-discipline and self-motivation are joined at the hip. Why is that? When you practice self-discipline you feel like you are in control of your life. You feel content and motivated because you're moving toward your goals.

On the other hand, psychologists tell us that stress and unhappiness arise when you feel controlled by outside circumstances, which is what happens when there is no discipline in your life. Author Brian Tracy is a friend, and one of the most disciplined people I've ever met. If fact, he is currently writing a book for us titled *The Power of Discipline*. He said, "Self-discipline is the key to personal greatness. It is the magic quality that opens doors for you and makes everything else possible. With self-discipline the average person can rise as far and as fast as his talents and intelligence can take him. But without self-discipline a person with every advantage of background, education and opportunity will seldom rise above mediocrity."

How high will you rise?

48

"The brick walls are not there to keep us out; the brick walls are there to give us a chance to show how badly we want something."

~Randy Pausch

Randy Pausch was 47 years old when he died from pancreatic cancer. He was, as the *Independent of London* put it, "the dying man who taught America how to live." His book, *The Last Lecture*, is an international best-seller and it offers many wonderful lessons about life.

Randy Pausch's "last lecture" was delivered in September, 2007, at Carnegie Mellon University, where he taught computer science. The lecture began with him standing before a screen beaming down chilling CT images of tumors in his liver, under the title *The Elephant in the Room*. He then said to a stunned audience, "I have about 6 months to live." He said, "I'm really in good shape, probably better shape than most of you," dropping to the floor to do push-ups.

He went on to say, "I'm dying and I'm having fun, and I'm going to keep having fun every day I have left." He talked about his childhood dreams and what they had taught him about life. He said, "If you live your life the right way, the karma will take care of itself...your dreams will come to you."

Randy Pausch really was a dying man who has taught America how to live.

He died on July 25, 2008, but his wisdom, his passion, and his attitude are lasting sources of inspiration for all of us.

49

"Think big...
start small...
move fast."

~ Bahram Akradi

About 2 miles from our office, in Naperville, Illinois, there is an excellent health club called LifeTime Fitness, to which I belong. They also have a monthly magazine called *Experience Life* that recently had a great article titled: **Think Big, Step Lightly.** It was written by their founder, Bahram Akradi, and I'd like to share a short excerpt on goals. Here's what he said:

When it comes to accomplishing personal goals, everyone has his or her own style. Some people like to tell the world what they're determined to achieve; others quietly commit their plans to the pages of journals they'll never show a soul.

Me? I've been known to do a little of both. But I've always experienced the most success in following the motto "Think big, start small, move fast." Here's why it works for me:

"Think big" *invites me to develop an ambitious and expansive enough vision to get excited about what I'm choosing to accomplish. Dull* *goals, after all, tend to make for dull and uninspired efforts. If I have the vague idea that I want to upgrade my fitness, for example, I set my sights on a concrete outcome – say, improving my triathlon bike time by a hefty percentage. My rule of thumb is this: If I can't see myself being totally thrilled about the success of the end accomplishment, I don't set is as a goal.*

"Start small" *saves me from getting overwhelmed by what I've taken on and lets me get started now, with modest daily actions that feel doable. Daily action equates with integrity and determination, in my view. You have to keep asking yourself: Do I really want this thing or not? Each day brings the opportunity to reconfirm your priorities and to move forward by doing something. Even if the action is just a single phone call, a few breaths on the yoga mat, or a swift left turn out of the snack aisle, it's still a step in the right direction and it builds momentum for more positive action.*

"Move fast" *gets me focused on making continual progress and keeps my energy and enthusiasm high. It prevents me from getting so bogged down in my daily actions that I lose sight of the big goal that got me excited in the first place. "Move fast" also keeps me honest about the kinds of mini-goals I'll need to accomplish in order to make meaningful headway. Most major goals are marathons, not sprints, so it's important to pace yourself. But part of pacing yourself is setting challenging (not impossible) interim goals – benchmarks that give you constant feedback about the progress you're making and that help you recognize where adjustments to your plan might be necessary. Because rapidly correcting errors is an essential part of this whole approach.*

As we know, your goals are critical to self-motivation, and Akradi offers some excellent "food for thought." He has a plan...do you?

"To love and be loved
is to feel the sun
from both sides."

~David Viscott

Not long ago, I received a letter from one of our customers. She said, "Mac, I love getting your newsletter and had to send you this beautiful story. I don't know who wrote it, but I hope you can find a way to share it with your customers."

I loved it, and thought it would be a great ending to a book about... "charging our own batteries." Thank you, Christine Benson, for sharing it with me!

3900 SATURDAYS

The older I get, the more I enjoy Saturday morning. Perhaps it's the quiet solitude that comes with being the first to rise, or maybe it's the unbounded joy of not having to be at work. Either way, the first few hours of a Saturday morning are most enjoyable.

A few weeks ago, I was shuffling toward the garage with a steaming cup of coffee in one hand and the morning paper in the other. What began as a typical Saturday morning turned into one of those lessons that life seems to hand you from time to time. Let me tell you about it:

I turned the dial up into the phone portion of the band on my ham radio in order to listen to a Saturday morning swap net. Along the way, I came across an older sounding chap, with a tremendous signal and a golden voice. You know the kind; he sounded like he should be in the broadcasting business. He was telling whomever he was talking with something about "a thousand marbles." I was intrigued and stopped to listen to what he had to say.

"Well, Tom, it sure sounds like you're busy with your job. I'm sure they pay you well but it's a shame you have to be away from home and your family so much. Hard to believe a young fellow should have to work sixty or seventy hours a week to make ends meet. It's too bad you missed your daughter's dance recital." He continued, "Let me tell you something that

has helped me keep my own priorities." And that's when he began to explain his theory of a "thousand marbles."

"You see, I sat down one day and did a little arithmetic. The average person lives about seventy-five years. I know, some live more and some live less, but on average, folks live about seventy-five years.

Now then, I multiplied 75 times 52 and I came up with 3,900, which is the number of Saturdays that the average person has in their entire lifetime. Now, stick with me, Tom, I'm getting to the important part.

It took me until I was fifty-five years old to think about all this in any detail," he went on, "and by that time I had lived through over twenty-eight hundred Saturdays. I got to thinking that if I lived to be seventy-five, I only had about a thousand of them left to enjoy. So I went to a toy store and bought every single marble they had. I ended up having to visit three toy stores to round up 1,000 marbles. I took them home and put them inside a large, clear plastic container right here in the shack next to my gear.

Every Saturday since then, I have taken one marble out and thrown it away. I found that by watching the marbles diminish, I focused more on the really important things in life.

There's nothing like watching your time here on this earth run out to help get your priorities straight.

Now let me tell you one last thing before I sign off with you and take my lovely wife out for breakfast. This morning, I took the very last marble out of the container. I figure that if I make it until next Saturday then I have been given a little extra time. And the one thing we can all use is a little more time.

It was nice to meet you, Tom. I hope you spend more time with your family, and I hope to meet you again here on the band. This is a 75 year old man, K9NZQ, clear and going QRT, good morning!"

You could have heard a pin drop on the band when this fellow signed off. I guess he gave us all a lot to think about. I had planned to work on the *antenna that morning, and then I was going to meet up with a few hams to work on the next club newsletter.*

Instead, I went upstairs and woke my wife up with a kiss. "C'mon honey, I'm taking you and the kids to breakfast."

"What brought this on?" she asked with a smile.

"Oh, nothing special, it's just been a long time since we spent a Saturday together with the kids. And hey, can we stop at a toy store while we're out? I need to buy some marbles."

"Enjoy the little things, for one day you may look back and realize they were the big things."

~Robert Brault

About the Author

Mac Anderson

MAC ANDERSON is the founder of Simple Truths and Successories, Inc., the leader in designing and marketing products for motivation and recognition. These companies, however, are not the fi rst success stories for Mac. He was also the founder and CEO of McCord Travel, the largest travel company in the Midwest, and part owner/VP of sales and marketing for Orval Kent Food Company, the country's largest manufacturer of prepared salads.

His accomplishments in these unrelated industries provide some insight into his passion and leadership skills. He also brings the same passion to his speaking where he speaks to many corporate audiences on a variety of topics, including leadership, motivation, and team building.

Mac has authored or co-authored twelve books that have sold over three million copies. His titles include:

- *Charging the Human Battery*
- *Customer Love*
- *Motivational Quotes*
- *Finding Joy*
- *You Can't Send a Duck to Eagle School*
- *212° : The Extra Degree*
- *Change is Good ... You Go First*
- *The Nature of Success*
- *The Power of Attitude*
- *The Essence of Leadership*
- *To a Child, Love is Spelled T-I-M-E*
- *The Dash*

For more information about Mac, visit www.simpletruths.com